The Life of a DOG

Clare Hibbert

Raintree
Chicago, Illinois

© Copyright 2004 Raintree
Published by Raintree, a division of Reed Elsevier, Inc.
Chicago, IL 60602
Customer Service 888-363-4266
Visit our website at www.raintreelibrary.com

For more information address the publisher:
Raintree, 100 N. LaSalle, Suite 1200, Chicago IL 60602

Printed and bound in China by the South China Printing Company

08 07 06
10 9 8 7 6 5 4 3 2

Library of Congress Cataloging-in-Publication Data:

Hibbert, Clare, 1970-
  Life of a dog / Clare Hibbert.
      p. cm. -- (Life cycles)
Summary: Describes the stages of a dog's life and how puppies learn various behaviors as they grow.
  ISBN 1-4109-0535-7 (hc), 1-4109-0923-9 (pbk)
  1. Dogs--Life cycles--Juvenile literature. [1. Dogs.]
I. Title. II.
Series: Life cycles (Chicago, Ill.)
  SF426.5.H53 2004
  636.7--dc21

                    2003006585

Acknowledgments
The publishers would like to thank the following for permission to reproduce photographs: pp. 4, 5, 8, 9, 10, 11, 12, 13, 14, 15, 16, 17, 18, 19, 20, 21, 23, 24, 25, 26, 27, 28, 29 Tudor Photography; p. 22 Richard Kolar/AA/Oxford Scientific Films.

Cover photograph of a young beagle, reproduced with permission of Oxford Scientific Films (Richard Kolar/AA)

The publishers would like to thank Janet Stott, and Veronica Bradley and Ken Burgess at Dufosee Kennels, Hereford, UK for their assistance in the preparation of this book.

Every effort has been made to contact copyright holders of any material reproduced in this book. Any omissions will be rectified in subsequent printings if notice is given to the publishers.

Contents

Any words appearing in the text in bold, **like this,** are explained in the Glossary.

The Dog

Dogs belong to a group of animals called **mammals.** You are a mammal, too. All mammals grow inside their mothers, and have hair or fur. Mammals suckle when they are born, meaning they drink milk from their mother's body.

Dogs are **pack** animals. Most wild dogs live and hunt in groups. A pet dog also belongs to a pack—its human family!

There are many different kinds, or breeds, of dog. The beagle is a popular pet breed.

Growing up

Just as you grow bigger year by year, a dog grows and changes, too. There are many different shapes and sizes of dog, but they all grow and change in the same stages. The different stages of the dog's life make up its **life cycle.**

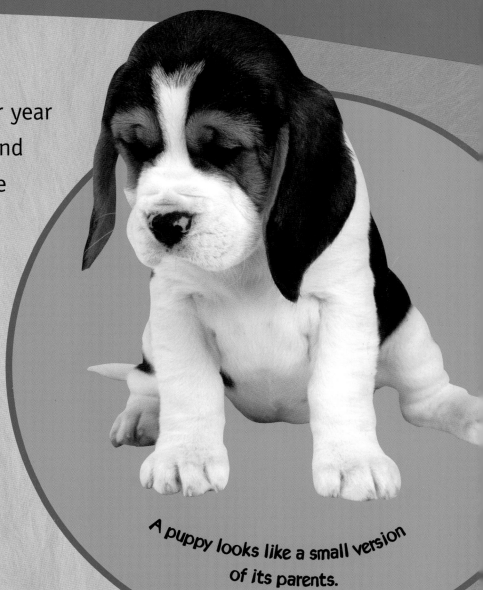

A puppy looks like a small version of its parents.

Where dogs live

Pet dogs live wherever there are people, in busy cities and on farms. Dogs' wild relatives include wolves, foxes, and jackals. Wild dogs live in just about every part of the world.

A Dog's Life

The **life cycle** of a dog begins when a male and female dog come together and **mate.** About 65 days later, the female dog gives birth to a **litter** of tiny, helpless baby dogs, called puppies.

A newborn puppy depends on its mother for milk and warmth. By three or four weeks, it is beginning to explore. The puppy can leave its mother at eight to twelve weeks. It can start having its own puppies when it is about six months old.

Last years

Pet dogs live for twelve to fourteen years and sometimes longer. As they get older, dogs sleep more. They do not need as much exercise or food.

A female dog is pregnant for around 65 days.

The newborn puppy is blind and helpless.

At two weeks, the puppy's eyes and ears open.

At four weeks, the puppy starts to play and eat solid food.

The puppy is allowed outside at twelve weeks (as long as it has had its **vaccinations**).

After they are six months, dogs are adults and can mate.

This diagram shows the life cycle of a dog, from newborn puppy to adult.

A Litter of Puppies

There are usually six or seven puppies in a **litter**, born about half an hour apart. Coming out into the cold world is a shock! As soon as each puppy is born, its mother licks it clean. A newborn puppy is small and helpless. It is unable to see or hear, because it cannot open its eyes or ears.

When the whole litter has been born, the mother lies on her side. The pups crawl toward her. Each one sniffs out a **teat** or nipple and takes a first drink of milk. This is called **suckling.**

A newborn puppy is small and weak. It cannot even open its eyes.

Daily life

For the first week, the puppies just sleep and feed. Their mother licks them, which gives them a shared, family smell. It also keeps them clean.

Body heat

Until the age of about three weeks, puppies cannot create enough of their own body heat to keep them warm. They snuggle up to their mother for warmth.

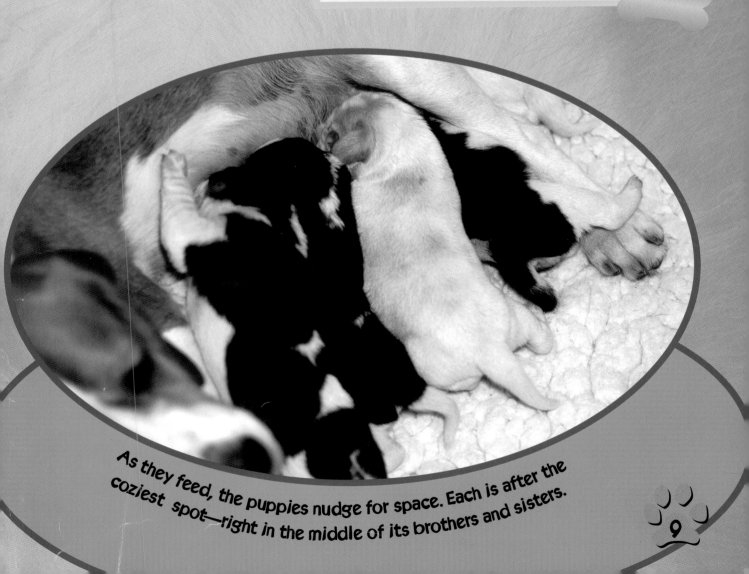

As they feed, the puppies nudge for space. Each is after the coziest spot—right in the middle of its brothers and sisters.

9

First Steps

After a week, the puppies are stronger. They are curious about the place where they were born. They use smell and touch to find their way. They crawl around because they are too wobbly to stand up.

These puppies are just a week old. They still need a lot of sleep.

Sights and sounds

The puppies' eyes and ears open when they are two weeks old. They can see and hear for the first time. They want to explore and play, but they soon get tired. Like human babies, puppies spend a lot of time asleep. They can also cry. Puppies whimper if they are afraid, cold, or hungry.

Puppy senses

Seeing, hearing, touching, smelling, and tasting are all senses. They tell you about the world. Dogs have senses, too. They are born with a good sense of smell, and can see and hear at two weeks. Their sensitive whiskers are used for touch and even for finding their way in the dark.

At just over two weeks old, the puppy is beginning to get its sense of balance. It can take a few steps without toppling over.

Hello World!

At three weeks old, the puppies start to notice what is going on around them. They try out new noises, such as barks and growls, and learn how other dogs respond to them. They also wag their tails for the first time.

Their mother keeps a close eye on the puppies. She bites them if they misbehave and stops them from wandering off.

These young puppies are eager to start exploring!

Baby food

The puppies still **suckle,** but their mother also gives them some of her own food, which she has chewed up. The puppies ask for this by licking their mother's mouth when she is eating.

Tail talk

Have you noticed how fast dogs can wag their tails? They do this to show they feel happy or playful. The tail is a way a dog shows how it is feeling. A tail hanging down between its legs could mean the dog is afraid, unhappy, or even sick.

By wagging its tail, a perky puppy can show that it feels friendly, happy, or that it wants to play.

13

Playtime

When they are a month old, the puppies begin to spend a lot more time playing. Being rough and tumbling with their brothers and sisters is a little like going to school for them. They pick up all the skills they will need as adult dogs.

One minute a pair of puppies might be sitting quietly... and the next, they will be playing chase!

Who's the boss?

The puppies have pretend fights with each other, where they can act out how to behave as the winner or the loser. They learn what sort of **body language** to use. The puppies even practice killer bites to the neck—but luckily their baby teeth are only just coming through so they don't hurt each other.

Through a lot of different kinds of play, the puppies learn their place in the **pack.** Pet dogs get to know their human owners better, too, and discover what to expect from them.

The growing puppies explore together. This toy looks like fun!

Meal Time

Puppies cannot leave their mothers until they stop **suckling.** The time it takes to do this is called **weaning.** It happens over a period of several weeks.

At a month old, the puppies' first tiny teeth appear. Now they can start to eat solid food. Dog owners usually start their puppies off on **gruel** first. This is like oatmeal and is easy for the puppies to eat and **digest.** Then the puppies move on to canned puppy food and small dog biscuits. Day by day, they take less milk from their mother and eat more solid food.

The puppy's teeth are sharp and pointy, just right for chewing meat.

Baby belly

Puppies need three or four small meals a day because their stomachs are too tiny to hold much food. Most adult dogs eat just one large meal a day.

Dog teeth

Puppies have 28 baby teeth. These fall out when the puppy is a few months old. They are replaced by 42 big, strong adult teeth. Dogs are meat eaters. Their teeth are designed for tearing and chewing.

These puppies are digging into some puppy food. Water is important for all dogs, but especially ones that eat dry foods.

A New Home

When the puppy is eight to twelve weeks old, it can leave its mother. Sometimes pet puppies go and live with new owners.

In its new home, the puppy does not have brothers and sisters to snuggle up to at night. This can be scary at first, but the puppy soon gets used to it.

A fresh start

Moving to its new house can be frightening for the young puppy. There are unfamiliar smells and strange sounds. There may even be other pets to meet. Slowly the puppy gets to know its new home and family. As the puppy gets used to its new home, the new owner trains the puppy so that it will grow up to be well behaved.

First lessons

The puppy soon recognizes commands such as "Sit!" and "Come!" When it obeys, it might get a reward, like a dog biscuit. The puppy learns another important lesson—where it is allowed to go to the bathroom.

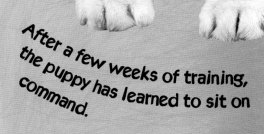
After a few weeks of training, the puppy has learned to sit on command.

Walks

Pet dogs cannot go outside until the vet has given them all their **vaccinations.** These protect against dog diseases. The last ones are given when a puppy is twelve weeks old. At last it can go for walks!

Young puppies have to learn how to walk obediently on a leash.

The great outdoors

Walks for a puppy are very exciting. The puppy must learn to greet other dogs with a polite sniff, not a jump, bark, or bite. It must walk calmly on a leash, even when it really wants to race off into the distance.

A walk is important exercise, as well as being an adventure. All dogs need exercise. It keeps them fit and healthy.

In woody areas and some parks, the puppy can run around off the leash.

Dangers

The biggest danger to a puppy outside is traffic. The puppy must be kept on a leash near streets and roads. Another problem, if it is allowed off a leash, is getting lost. In warm weather the puppy could overheat without enough shade and water.

Growing Up

Between the ages of 14 and 26 weeks, the puppy starts to lose its baby teeth. Owners often do not even notice, because the teeth are usually just swallowed.

Body fuel

Now the puppy's strong adult teeth start to come through. The puppy's body looks more grown up, too. All this growing can make the puppy very hungry.

This beagle is four months old. It has almost finished growing and already has its adult teeth and coat.

The owner starts to give the puppy fewer, larger meals. By the time it is nine months old, the dog is eating two large meals a day.

Coat

A puppy's coat is soft to the touch. Adult dogs have a double coat. They have a soft undercoat of puppylike fur and then a tough top layer of bristly, waterproof hairs. These start to appear when the puppy is about three months old.

At nine months, the dog's stomach is big enough to get by on two meals a day.

Territory

In the wild, dog **packs** have an area of land where they live and hunt. This is their **territory.** They do not want to share the land with other packs, so they leave signs that tell other dogs to stay away. The signs are all smells.

When they meet each other, dogs sniff each other's bodies. It is their way of saying hello.

Nose know how

Pet dogs mark their territory, too, with smelly scent messages. That is what a dog is doing when it goes to the bathroom against a tree or hydrant. It also picks up all the scents left behind by other dogs. A dog can even smell where another dog's footprints were.

Fleas

Fleas are **insect** pests that can live on dogs. Like all living things, fleas have their own **life cycle.** Flea **grubs** hatch from eggs, then grow and change into adults. Fleas bite dogs to feed on their blood. Dogs catch fleas from being where other dogs have been.

Dogs start to mark their territory when they are eight to twelve months old.

Pairing Up

A female dog can have puppies from the age of six months. First, she must **mate** with a male dog. The two dogs come together to make the puppies. The pups grow inside their mother for 65 days. While they are growing inside her, they are called **embryos.**

This female dog is lying down. This tells the male that she is willing to mate with him.

Swollen

The embryos need energy to grow, so the female eats extra food. During the last few weeks you can start to tell she is **pregnant.** The embryos have grown big enough to make her belly stick out.

No pups

Most pet dogs are **neutered,** meaning they have an operation so that they will not be able to have babies. This is because there are already too many unwanted puppies in the world.

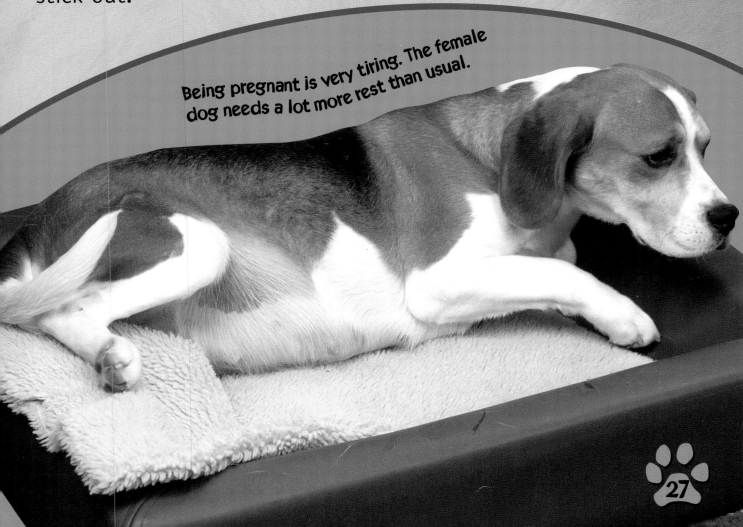

Being pregnant is very tiring. The female dog needs a lot more rest than usual.

New Life

When it is time for the dog to have her pups, she looks for a quiet place. Even if she has never had puppies before, she knows just what to do. Each puppy is born inside a bag of skin, which the mother must tear through with her teeth. Next, she bites through the **umbilical cord.** This cord carried food to the puppy **embryos.**

This mother's first litter cuddle up for a drink.

A new beginning

It takes three or four hours for all her pups to be born. Now the mother lies on her side so the pups can **suckle,** just like she did when she was a puppy. With each of these newborn pups, the **life cycle** can start all over again.

This newborn might be helpless now, but it will soon grow up.

29

Find Out for Yourself

The best way to find out more about the life cycle of a dog is to watch it happen with your own eyes. Pet dogs are a big responsibility, though, so you should only get one if you are sure you have the time to care for it.

Books to read

Head, Honor. *My Pet: Puppy*. Chicago: Raintree, 2000.

Powell, Jillian. *How Do They Grow? From Puppy To Dog*. Chicago: Raintree, 2001.

Using the Internet
Explore the Internet to find out more about dogs. Websites can change, and if some of the links below no longer work, don't worry. Use a search engine, such as www.yahooligans.com, and type in keywords such as "dog," "puppy," and "life cycle."

Websites
http://www.dogshome.org/playtime
Play games, watch video clips about taking care of a dog, or spoil your pup with one of the special doggy recipes!
http://www.rspca.org.uk
Choose "Dog" from "Animal Care" to find out everything you need to know about taking care of a pet dog.

Glossary

body language   way the body's action or pose gives out a message

digest   pass food through the body, taking all its nutrition on the way

embryo   baby animal before it has been born or hatched

grub   young insect that looks nothing like its parent. Adult insects have six legs. Grubs usually have none.

gruel   food made with oats and warm water

insect   animal that, as an adult, has three parts to its body, three pairs of legs, and usually two pairs of wings. Fleas and bees are insects.

life cycle   all the different stages in the life of a living thing

litter   group of baby animals that are all born to the same mother at the same time

mammal   animal that has fur or hair, and that gives birth to its young and feeds them on milk

mate   when a male and female animal come together to make eggs or babies

neutered   animal that has had an operation so that it will not be able to have babies

obedient   well behaved and good at following commands

pack   name for a group of dogs that live and hunt together

pregnant   when a female has a baby growing inside her body

suckle   drink a mother's milk

teat   mother animal's nipple, where milk comes from for her babies to drink

territory   area of land where an animal or a group of animals lives. Animals often mark their territory by leaving their scent, which warns other animals to stay away.

umbilical cord   tube that links a baby mammal to its mother while it is growing inside her. The cord carries food and oxygen to the baby.

vaccination   injection that helps the body to fight off a certain disease

weaning   getting a baby animal to stop drinking its mother's milk and start eating solid foods

Index